# An Introduction to Organ Registration

**James Engel**

**Church Music Pamphlet Series**
**Carl Schalk, Editor**

Publishing House
St. Louis

# Contents

Introduction                                                          3
A Summary of the Overtone Phenomenon                                  6
The Classification of Organ Registers According to Pitch              9
The Classification of Organ Tone According to Timbre                 12
The Art of Registration: Combining Registers                         16
Further Considerations on the Disposition of Registers               28
Mechanical Registrational Devices                                    36
Appendix A                                                           38
Appendix B                                                           41
Bibliography                                                         47

Copyright © 1986 Concordia Publishing House
3558 S. Jefferson Avenue, St. Louis, MO 63118-3968
Manufactured in the United States of America

Library of Congress Cataloging in Publication Data

Engel, James.
    An introduction to organ registration.

    (Church music pamphlet series)
    Bibliography: p.
    1. Organ—Registration. I. Title. II. Series.
MT189.E53 1986        786.6        86-11721
ISBN 0-570-01334-8

1 2 3 4 5 6 7 8 9 10  MID  95 94 93 92 91 90 89 88 87 86

# Introduction

Timbre, cohesive ensemble, intensity, and balance are but a few of the extremely important factors an orchestral conductor considers prior to the performance of a musical score. Controlling nuances of color and balance within the orchestral ensemble presents no small task even to the most experienced conductor. His aim is to bring to life an otherwise lifeless score so as to provide an avenue of communication through tone between composer and listener. As such, the conductor serves both composer and listener in that unique position within the arts—a performer. Whereas in the other fine arts the creator communicates directly with his public, music alone must ever be created anew for the listener by means of a "re-creator"—the performer.

Though an intermediary position, the role of performer is nevertheless extremely demanding, requiring much time and training and a high degree of musicianship. Contemporary notation systems being what they are, it is virtually impossible for the composer to indicate all matters of balance, timbre, or intensity exactly as he originally conceived them. Consequently, in the art of music much is left to the taste, the understanding, and the musical discretion of the performer.

The orchestral conductor, as a responsible performer, begins with a careful examination of the score, for his primary task will be to determine the composer's intentions concerning every musical detail completely from the symbols within the composer's notation.

The successful conductor not only is concerned with instrumental ranges and general family characteristics but also becomes deeply involved with relative intensities of the solo instruments, balance within the ensemble, the blending of colors, and so forth in his search for the ultimate clarity and precision that the composer's work deserves. The conductor will, of course, be as faithful to the printed score as he can be. But in almost every score there will be instances when the conductor, sensing the intentions of the composer, will feel

3

the need to adapt the original scoring to his particular situation—the orchestra at his disposal, the performance area in which the work will be performed, etc.

Although managing color and balance are but a part of the conductor's total leadership responsibilities, his manipulation of these factors alone requires a great deal of theoretical preparation, first-hand experience with all the instruments, and a fine aural sense of tonal balance, among other things.

In many respects the organist, as a performer, faces the same challenges that an orchestral conductor encounters. He, too, has a responsibility to the composer of the work he performs as well as to his audience. The considerations of a practicing organist extend far beyond the mere recognition of registers and families of stops. The real art of organ registration includes a fine understanding of the timbres of all the individual ranks of pipes throughout their ranges and a sure grasp of the vast array of ensemble possibilities within the instrument at hand. The organist's primary purpose, like the orchestral conductor's, is to bring to the listener the composer's perceived intentions as well as he can with whatever means are at his disposal, adapting, if necessary, the composer's registrational outlines to his own instrument and to the acoustical perculiarities of the place in which the music will be played and heard.

The organist should gain this ability first through an understanding of the fundamental acoustical concepts concerning organ sound. Some of these matters will be reviewed on the following pages. To this should be added, however, a great deal of experimentation with the tonal resources of the organist's own instrument and of any other organ to which he can gain access. In addition he must possess a fine sense of discrimination of the formal structure of the compositions that may affect registrational procedures.

One of the most frustrating problems facing the amateur organist as he approaches the matter of registration is the rather obvious "confusion of tongues" in the instruments he hears and plays. He soon becomes aware that the organ, more than any other instrument, lacks standardization. What constitutes fine organ tone and excellence in organ ensemble has changed dramatically over the centuries since the first organs were built. In addition to this, the organist, bent on learning good tonal principles, soon realizes that many instruments 75 to 100 years old and more are still in use. These older instruments, oversupplied with 8' ranks and often lacking in "upper work," represent concepts of organ building now long forsaken. (The reader might well be responsible for regular performance on one of these instruments.) Even within the last 50 years, a time of renaissance in organ building, wide differences among the foremost organ builders are still evident in the formulation of organ tone both in individual registers and in the ensemble of the instrument. Some leading organ builders have also altered drastically their own methods of construction over the years so that their early instruments sound considerably different than those built more recently. One might also discover that a reliable builder has constructed 8' Principals, for example, of considerably different tonal character for two different churches simply because the acoustical properties of the two buildings are significantly different.

Nevertheless, despite all these divergencies in existing instruments, the art of organ building within this century has made great strides forward. Forsaking the Romantic notion that the organ ought to reproduce orchestral sonorities, most builders today have adopted the more classical view: that the organ is truly an instrument in its own right with its unique tonal character, function, and repertoire. Modern organ builders have made greater efforts to construct instruments according to principles followed by the respected organ builders of the 17th and 18th centuries. Greater efforts are being made today to design and build organs specifically adapted to the building in which the instrument is to sound. The acoustical properties of the building, which may range from very live to very "dry," are a vital part of the organ itself. Conscientious organ builders design and construct every rank—in reality, every pipe—for the very room in which it will sound.

# A Summary of the Overtone Phenomenon

An overview of the natural overtone phenomenon is a prerequisite for an understanding of the traditional pitch numbering system used on most organs. Most vibrating bodies that produce musical pitch follow similar natural principles. It can best be explained in terms of vibrating strings.

When a string vibrates, it naturally and simultaneously vibrates as a whole and in halves, thirds, fourths, fifths, and so on. The vibration of the entire string as a unit is called the fundamental vibration and produces the fundamental pitch—the pitch most easily identified by ear. Each of the fractional parts of the string vibrates at faster speeds, each fractional part producing its own definable pitch above the fundamental. These smaller vibrations are termed harmonics, or overtones. The term "partial" refers to any one of the individual parts of the entire system, including the fundamental (the first partial). (See Chart I, p.7)

In explanation of Chart I, when a taut string (a) is plucked, it vibrates as a whole (b), in halves (c), in thirds (d), and in many more of its exact fractional parts (e, f, g, h, i) until it naturally returns to its original state of rest (a). All of these vibrations are produced simultaneously, a natural fact that is difficult to conceive and difficult to diagram. Each of these vibrations, fundamental and harmonic, continues throughout the entire length of the string without interfering with each other.

The vibration of the entire string (b) is the widest (has the greatest amplitude), makes the greatest impression on our ear, and is therefore most easily distinguished. The amplitude of each succeeding fractional vibration is successively narrower, making less impact on our ear, and is thus less audible. Nevertheless, these overtones are extremely important in providing quality, characteristic color to the entire tonal spectrum that we hear.

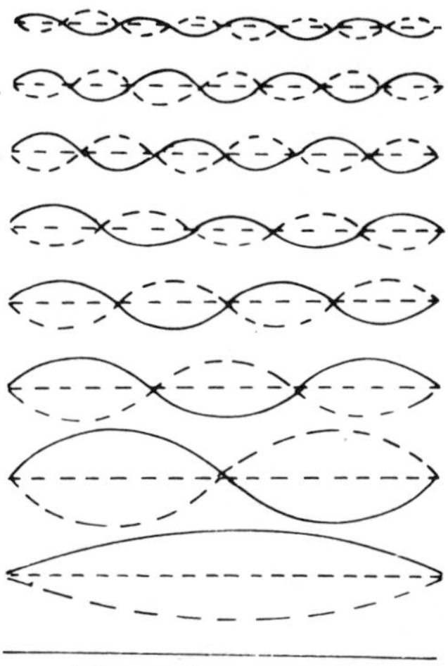

| A. Wave patterns of a vibrating string 8′ in length showing the first eight harmonics. Dotted curved lines show the position ½ cycle later. | B. Length of the vibrating segment whole = 8′ | C. Overtone produced | D. Partial | E. Relative pitch produced if fundamentalis C. | F. Relativespeed of vibration |
|---|---|---|---|---|---|
| i. | $\frac{8}{8} = 1'$ | 7 | 8 | c″ | 512 |
| h. | $\frac{8}{7} = 1\frac{1}{7}'$ | 6 | 7 | b′ | 448 |
| g. | $\frac{8}{6} = 1\frac{1}{3}'$ | 5 | 6 | g′ | 384 |
| f. | $\frac{8}{5} = 1\frac{3}{5}'$ | 4 | 5 | e′ | 320 |
| e. | $\frac{8}{4} = 2'$ | 3 | 4 | c′ | 256 |
| d. | $\frac{8}{3} = 2\frac{2}{3}'$ | 2 | 3 | g | 194 |
| c. | $\frac{8}{2} = 4'$ | 1 | 2 | c | 128 |
| b. | $\frac{8}{1} = 8'$ | funda-mental | 1 | C | 64 |
| a. The string at rest | | | | | |

**Chart I — Harmonic Analysis of a Vibrating String***

* From Charles Luedtke, *Fundamentals of Organ Registration*

Each of the fractional parts (c, d, e, etc.) produces a successively faster vibration and therefore a higher pitch. All these fractional pitches are exact multiples of the fundamental vibration. Thus if the fundamental is moving at 64 vibrations per second, the second partial will vibrate at 128, the third at 192 (3 × 64), the fourth at 256 (4 × 64) (see column F). The individual pitches above C (64 vibrations per second) are given in column E.

If the entire string (a) is 8′ in length, the exact fractional parts (½, ⅓, ¼, ⅕, etc.) will have respectively shorter lengths:

½ vibration (× 8), each part will be 4′
⅓ vibration (× 8), each part will be 2⅔′
¼ vibration (× 8), each part will be 2′
See columns A and B.

Almost all vibrating bodies, including air in an enclosed column as in organ pipes, produce fundamental and overtones naturally in a similar manner. The overtones are mathematically and musically related to their fundamental. The same relative pattern of overtones exists regardless of the pitch of the fundamental. The first overtone will always be one octave higher, the second overtone an octave and a fifth higher, the third two octaves higher, etc. (see Chart II, p. 8).

### The pattern of fundamentals and overtones (octaves and mutations) indicating relative pitches

| | | Harmonic Series | | | |
|---|---|---|---|---|---|
| Stop in feet | Pitch in relation to note played | 16' | 8' | 4' | 2' |
| 16' | One octave lower | 1st | | | |
| 10⅔' | A perfect fourth lower | | | | |
| 8' | NORMAL PITCH OF NOTE PLAYED | 2d | 1st | | |
| 5⅓' | A perfect fifth higher | 3rd | | | |
| 4' | One octave higher | 4th | 2d | 1st | |
| 3⅕' | One octave and a third higher | 5th | | | |
| 2⅔' | One octave and a fifth higher | 6th | 3rd | | |
| 2' | Two octaves higher | 8th | 4th | 2d | 1st |
| 1⅗' | Two octaves and a third higher | 10th | 5th | | |
| 1⅓' | Two octaves and a fifth higher | 12th | 6th | 3rd | |
| 1⅐' | Two octaves and a seventh higher | 14th | 7th | | |
| 1' | Three octaves higher | 16th | 8th | 4th | 2d |

### Chart II — Harmonic Analysis of Organ Pitches *

\* From Flor Peeters, *Ars Organi.* Brusselles: Schott Freres. Part I. adapted

# The Classification of Organ Registers According to Pitch

A "stop" signifies a rank, a set of pipes of similar construction and material and therefore similar quality of sound. The term is also used to mean the tab or knob that puts a rank of pipes into action. In early mechanical organs such a knob, when pushed in, actually stopped the flow of air into the chest below the rank of pipes, hence the term *stop.* Today *register* is used synonymously with *stop.*

A stop tab or draw knob may put into readiness a single set of pipes (a rank) with one pipe for each key. Certain stop tabs or draw knobs will bring on two or more sets of pipes that will sound simultaneously. These registers or stops are known as mutations ($2\frac{2}{3}'$, $1\frac{3}{5}'$, $1\frac{1}{3}'$) or mixtures (II, III, IV, V).

Eight-foot ($8'$) stops are unison or standard-pitched stops. In an $8'$ set of open pipes the lowest (and therefore the longest) pipe is eight feet in length.[1] The fundamental pitch of an $8'$ rank sounds the actual notated pitch. Were we to limit organs to only $8'$ ranks of pipes, the tone of the ensemble would indeed be dull and heavy.

Organ pipes, especially Gedackts and Flutes, due to the simplicity of their construction, have weak overtone systems when compared to most orchestral instruments. The overtone structure of any musical tone imparts to that tone its peculiar color, its unique quality. The weaker overtones of the $8'$ ranks are greatly enhanced in the organ by separate sets of pipes. The higher pitched ranks ($4'$, $2\frac{2}{3}'$, $2'$, $1\frac{3}{5}'$, $1\frac{1}{3}'$, and $1'$), when drawn singly or in combination in addition to the fundamental $8'$ rank, supply a wide variety of differing timbres by emphasizing one or more of the overtones. These upper ranks, which correspond to the natural overtones above a fundamental (see Chart

---

[1]This and all future references to lowest pipe lengths are expressed with approximate accuracy. There are many variations from the stated length due to different pipe constructions, voicings, wind pressures, etc.

I, p. 7), add color, richness, and brilliance to the fundamental 8' rank.

*The Octave Pitches.* The lowest note of a 4' rank is produced by a pipe that is four feet long. The entire 4' rank, note for note, will sound one octave higher than the 8' rank throughout the entire range of the keyboard. The 4' rank reinforces the first overtone of the open 8' rank.

The lowest open pipe in a 2' rank is 2' long. The 2' rank of pipes will provide tones an octave higher than the 4' set, two octaves above the 8' set. The 2' rank reinforces the third overtone of an open 8' rank.

A 16' rank of pipes will produce pitches one octave below the 8' rank. It will sound pitches one octave below notated pitch. These ranks are used to reinforce bass lines in much the same manner as the string bass in an orchestra doubles the violoncello one octave lower.

The Gedackts (Stopped Diapason), or covered pipes, because of certain acoustical laws, produce pitches about one octave lower than their apparent length. Thus a covered or stopped pipe four feet in actual length will emit an 8' fundamental pitch. Despite its real physical length, it is labeled 8' on the stop tab at the console.

*The Mutations.* Mutation stops also reinforce the natural harmonics of fundamental ranks. The mutation ranks include those harmonics that are non-octave pitches. These are the second, fourth, fifth, and sixth overtones of a fundamental pitch.

The 2⅔' stop activates a rank of pipes one-third the length of those producing an 8' pitch. The 2⅔' rank supplies the third overtone, an octave and a fifth above the fundamental.

A 1⅗' stop activates a rank of pipes one-fifth the length of those producing 8' pitch. The 1⅗' rank reinforces the fourth overtone of an open 8' rank, two octaves and a third above the fundamental 8' pitch.

A 1⅓' stop activates a rank of pipes one-sixth the length of those producing 8' pitch. The 1⅓' rank reinforces the fifth overtones, two octaves and a fifth above the fundamental 8' pitch.

The 1' stop activates a rank of pipes one-eighth the length of those producing 8' pitch. The 1' rank reinforces the eighth overtone of an open 8' rank, three octaves above the fundamental 8' pitch.

All mutation stops are labeled as mixed numbers and sound pitches that are never in unison with or at octaves with the fundamental. By changing the mixed number of a mutation stop to an improper fraction one can easily determine the partial of the fundamental that is reinforced by that stop. Thus, since $2\frac{2}{3} = \frac{8}{3}$, the $2\frac{2}{3}'$ rank will sound the third partial of an 8′ fundamental. Since $5\frac{1}{3} = \frac{16}{3}$, the $5\frac{1}{3}'$ rank will sound the third partial of a 16′ fundamental (see Chart II, p. 8).

*The Mixtures.* Two, three, or more ranks activated by a single stop tab or draw knob are a mixture. Mixtures are likewise tuned to natural harmonics above a fundamental. Mixtures usually have from three to five ranks, though at times on larger instruments mixtures of 8 or 10 ranks are available. Quint mixtures are most common. These are made up of octaves and fifths only. A four-rank mixture might then include G-C-G-C, the 19th, 22d, 26th, and 29th notes above low C on the keyboard. Depending on the relative strengths of the individual ranks, mixtures can be designed to reinforce a Principal chorus or a reed chorus.

The number of ranks controlled by the mixture stop tab is usually indicated with a Roman numeral. Thus a III on the stop tab would indicate a mixture of three different ranks. Occasionally the pitch of the lowest sounding pipe is also indicated on the stop tab. A Mixture III $1\frac{1}{3}'$ would then include

a $1\frac{1}{3}'$ rank sounding two octaves and a fifth above the fundamental,

a 1′ rank sounding three octaves above the fundamental, and

a $\frac{2}{3}'$ rank sounding three octaves and a fifth above the fundamental.

# The Classification of Organ Tone According to Timbre

Over the centuries, a great number of labels have been used on stop tabs. By such labels the organ builder intends to indicate something of the color, tonal character, or pitch of the rank that is controlled by that stop tab. Despite the great variety of such names, all ranks of pipes fall into a few general categories or families. All registers can be listed in one of four general categories on the basis of tone color, which in turn depends on the structure of the pipe, the shape of the air column, and the means of initiating the vibration. Each of the four families—Principals, Flutes and Gedackts, Strings, and Reeds—will be discussed separately.

A broader yet extremely important distinction, contrasting basic organ tone with characteristic organ tone, is called to our attention by Carl Halter:

> Under basic organ tone [Principals and Flutes] we have included such stops as are historically indigenous to the organ only, and compared to which the reeds and strings are only additives. Characteristic tone is usually used not in the basic organ ensemble but for added color and as an addition to, and foil for, the basic color of the organ. Pipes in this class tend not to blend easily with pipes in the basic organ tone. They are constructed and voiced with a view toward producing a unique, singular tone that generally is sufficient unto itself and resists combination. Often these pipes imitate orchestral instruments either of the present or of more ancient times.[1]

Flue pipes are common to three of the families mentioned above. The vibration within a flue pipe is initiated by the impact of a stream of air directed against a relatively sharp metal or wooden edge at the upper lip of the mouth of the pipe. These are also called labial pipes.

[1]Carl Halter, The Practice of Sacred Music (St. Louis: Concordia Publishing House, 1955), p 69.

In contrast, the initiation of tone in the lingual pipes (reed family) is brought about by the impact of a stream of air against a flexible metal tongue within the foot of the pipe.

*Principals.* The Principal family supplies the fundamental or characteristic tone of the organ. Principals provide an aggressive firmness to registration combinations. The timbre of stops belonging to the Principal family is characterized by a fine balance between fundamental and overtone structure (see Appendix B, p. 41). The pipes in this category have moderate diameters; they are open and cylindrical and most often have a high tin content.

Principal ranks in combination provide excellent support for the congregation in the singing of hymns and liturgy. They are often used in both polyphonic and homophonic compositions that require firm tone and volume ranges from mezzo forte to fortissimo.

Principal, Diapason, Open Diapason, Montre 16', 8', 4', 2'
Octave, Super Octave, Fifteenth 4', 2', 1'
Twelfth, Quint 2⅔', 1⅓' (not to be confused with the Nazard)
Mixture, Fourniture, Scharf, Plein Jeu, Zimbel II, III, IV, V

*Flutes and Gedackts.* In the discussion that follows this rather large family will be further subdivided into three separate categories: Open Flutes, Covered Flutes (Gedackts), and Partially Covered Flutes.

As a family, the Flutes and Gedackts are generally more yielding in tonal color—considerably less aggressive than the Principals—due to a somewhat restricted overtone structure over a rather prominent fundamental. The pipes in this family generally have wider diameters and are either cylindrical or conical in shape. The Open Flutes are somewhat brighter and have a rather strong first overtone. The Gedackts are duller with the second overtone more prominent than the first (see Appendix B, p. 41).

*The Open Flutes*
Concert Flute, Melodia 8'
Spitzfloete, Hohlfloete 8', 4'
Harmonic Flute 4'
Nachthorn, Blockfloete 4', 2'
Waldfloete, Piccolo, Flautino 2'
Mutations—constructed to reinforce the non-octave overtones
    Nazard, Nasat 2⅔'

Terz, Tierce 1⅗′
Klein Nasat, Larigot 1⅓′
Septieme 1⅐′

*The Gedackts*
Subbass, Lieblich Gedackt, Quintaton 16′
Bourdon, Stopped Diapason, Gedackt 8′
Quintadena, Quintade 8′

*Partially Covered Flutes*
Rohrfloete, Rohrgedackt 8′, 4′
Koppelfloete, Spillfloete 4′

The Gedackts and the Partially Covered Flutes are especially usable as accompanying timbres. They also serve very well as foundation ranks for larger combinations including mutations and/or Principals.

*Strings.* The number and variety of stops in the String family is quite limited. This family is most notably associated with the music of the Romantic period. String ranks are occasionally omitted entirely from smaller instruments. Though the dynamic level of the ranks in the String family generally ranges between mezzo piano and piano, their timbre is keen, precise, and even harsh at times. The narrow pipe work provides a full array of upper harmonics over a weak fundamental (see Appendix B, p. 41).

Gambe, Salicional, Dolce, Viola, Viole 8′
Celeste, Vox Celeste 8′
Violina 4′
Gemshorn 8′

The Celeste ranks are purposely tuned slightly above pitch so as to create an undulating effect when used in conjunction with a well-tuned Salicional. This is done to simulate the string section of an orchestra. The Celeste, therefore, is never used alone or with any rank other than the Salicional. The Strings do not combine well with other ranks. They are not used with Principals or in larger combinations. Occasionally the Salicional is used with a 4′ Flute or with a 2⅔′ Nazard to serve as a quiet solo against a Gedackt 8′ background.

The Gemshorn and the Erzahler are hybrids with tone colors somewhere between flute and string tone. On some instruments they may be scaled to sound somewhat like flutes, on others like strings.

*Reeds.* All lingual pipes are classified together in the reed family of registers. The tone of the lingual pipe is produced by a vibrating reed set into motion by a steady stream of air through the boot of the pipe. Reed pipes generally have nasal, pungent timbres. A wide variety of reed stops has been incorporated into organs over the centuries. Their tone quality might range from very mild to extremely brilliant. The size and shape of the reed and the resonator, as well as the wind pressure, all play an important part in focusing and emphasizing selected harmonics, which accounts for the wide array of timbres in this family. The dynamic level may range from mezzo piano to fortissimo.

Bombarde, Posaune 32', 16'

Sordun, Rankett 16'

Fagott 16', 8', 4'

Trompette, Trumpet 16', 8', 4'

Schalmey, Oboe, Cromorne, Krummhorn, Cornopean 8'

Regal 8', 4'

Clarion, Rohrschalmei 4'

Less popular with contemporary organ builders are the "orchestral" reeds. The Clarinet, French Horn, English Horn, Bassoon, and Orchestral Oboe are seldom included in organ specifications today. Their unique timbres, purposely designed to imitate orchestral instruments, blended poorly when combined with other organ registers. Far more versatile are the classically designed Schalmeys or Krummhorns. They sound equally well as solo reeds or in combination with upper octaves and mutations.

# The Art of Registration: Combining Registers

The primary task of the organist as a performer is to bring to the listener the full impact of the music of the composer. The organist in performance will recreate as clearly and sensitively as possible the composer's intentions, be that of tempo, rhythm, phrasing, accent, nuance, or color (registration). To achieve an appropriate registration for a composition, the organist begins by considering the following:

—The composer's suggested registration (if there is one)
—The acoustical properties of the room
—The resources available in the instrument
—The content and form of the composition to be performed
—In the case of a "period" composition, the tonal concepts current at the time of the composition, realizing that there existed a traditional "sound".

Since organs lack standardization in specifications or designed registers, a composer's suggested registrations must often be modified. If a suggested stop is not available, substitutions should be made from the ranks within the same family of stops as listed above. An Oboe perhaps must be substituted for a suggested Schalmey, a Stopped Diapason for a Holz Gedackt.

The organist who must regularly perform in an acoustically "dry" church replete with wall-to-wall carpeting and seat cushions might do well to brighten suggested combinations. An 8′ Gedackt and 4′ Octave suggested by the composer might better be altered to 8′ Gedackt, 4′ Rohrfloete, and 2′ Principal. On the other hand, in a very "live" building an 8′ Gedackt and 4′ Flute could well be closer to the composer's intention. Furthermore, modification will be necessary if what is evidently a balanced combination on the composer's instrument sounds out of proportion and balance on the instrument at the performer's disposal. The organist should view the composer's registrations as

16

suggestions that must be adapted to the instrument at hand. Substitution and adjustment based on the content of the composition are routine procedures for the church organist.

Especially in the case of chorale preludes it will be of considerable value for the performer to ponder the text as well as to examine the texture of the composition before considering tempo, registration, and style. One assumes that the composer's primary intention in writing a chorale prelude was to establish the underlying mood in which the chorale might be sung, not simply to set a tempo or to set out the tune. The chorale text then might to some degree suggest and/or limit the registrational color as well as the tempo and general style of performance. Registration in all organ music should serve the composition, its form and its content.

A careful perusal of organ music with an eye to form and construction reveals that there are but four registrational requirements. Within these four general areas, however, are many possibilities. It will be well for the organist to begin with these general categories, which in turn will guide the selection of appropriate specific combinations, whatever the size of the instrument.

1. A single melody line (in any voice part range) may be of such prime importance that it demands more attention and therefore soloistic treatment and rendition by a *Solo Registration.*
2. Solo lines (whether played on a special organ registration, sung by a vocalist, or performed on a solo instrument) most often are accompanied by a *Background Registration.*
3. Many polyphonic organ compositions require a mixed-tone combination of registers. In this type of composition no single part of the texture is intended to be emphasized above any of the other parts. So that all the voices are "colored" equally, both hands remain on the same manual. Likewise, in many homophonically conceived compositions in which the melody line (the highest sounding voice) is supported by a chordal structure requiring both hands on the same manual, a mixed-tone combination of stops is drawn called a *Plenum Registration.*
4. In those organ compositions composed of two or three parts throughout, in which all parts are independent and relatively

equal melodically and rhythmically, the organist selects a *Duo* or *Trio Registration.*

Before discussing each of these registration possibilities in detail it will be appropriate to state first some rather basic concepts that will apply throughout.

Since 8′ ranks provide the standard (notated) pitch, the organist may assume that unless otherwise indicated by the composer, at least one 8′ stop should be drawn on each manual and in the pedal. Unless otherwise directed by the composer, a 16′ pedal stop will be drawn together with a suitable 8′ rank. The 16′ pedal rank with the 8′ corresponds to the common orchestral practice of duplicating the violoncello (bass) part one octave lower with the string bass.

To attain clarity, it is best to restrict registration combinations to but *one* rank of a given pitch level: *one* 8′ pitch, *one* 4′ pitch, and so on, selecting one of each pitch level until the desired intensity and breadth is reached. Whether to draw a strong 8′, medium 8′, or weaker 8′ will be determined by the type and content of the composition (see examples in Charts III, IV, V, Appendix A, pp. 38-40).

*Solo Registration.* Emphasis on a single voice in a musical texture might be achieved in any of the following ways:

1. By placement. The composer assigns the melody to the uppermost voice.
2. By speed. The composer assigns faster note values to a single voice part while all the other voices move more deliberately.
3. By volume. The organist achieves soloistic effect by assigning a louder stop or combination (on a separate manual) to the solo voice.
4. By timbre. The organist achieves soloistic effect by assigning a distinctive color to the melody.

The solo effect in the first two cases is compositionally achieved by the composer. The solo effect in the third and fourth cases makes special registrational demands on the performer.

On smaller instruments a solo effect is sometimes only possible by assigning a louder stop to the voice to be emphasized. For example, one might accompany an 8′ Diapason (Open) with an 8′ Gedackt or 8′ Stopped Diapason. More satisfying and surely more artistic results are achieved when the solo voice is assigned a distinctive color. This

18

may be done through the use of individual ranks, especially con-structed for their "character" sound:

| Manuals I or II | | Pedal | |
|---|---|---|---|
| Trumpet | 8' | Fagott | 16' |
| Krummhorn | 8' | Trumpet | 8' |
| Fagott | 8' | Clarion | 4' |
| Regal | 8' | Rohr Schalmey | 4' |
| Oboe | 8' | | |
| Schalmey | 8' | | |
| Cornopean | 8' | | |

It should be noted that the pedal at times carries the solo voice. If the solo is really to be a bass solo, an 8' reed (with the possible 16' addition of a stop) is required. If in fact that pedal is assigned a solo in the soprano or alto range, a 4' pedal solo reed is necessary (see examples).

The use of a manual reed as solo is especially suited to slower moving solos (longer note values) or inner voice (alto or tenor) solos.

A synthetic solo registration consists of a combination of two or more ranks of the flue family of differing pitches. The combination would have an 8' foundation stop, normally of the Gedackt or Flute families, plus one or more of the higher flue ranks: 4', 2⅔', 2', 1⅗', 1⅓', or 1'. Occasionally a gentle Principal, Gemshorn, or Salicional at 8' pitch will supply the necessary fundamental pitch.

Gedackt 8' plus Piccolo 2'
Gedackt 8' plus Nazard 2⅔'
Diapason 8' plus Nazard 2⅔'
Salicional 8' plus Nazard 2⅔'
Gedackt 8' plus Nazard 2⅔' plus Piccolo 2'
Gedackt 8' plus Nazard 2⅔' plus Tierce 1⅗'
Salicional 8' plus Flute 4' plus Tierce 1⅗'
Gemshorn 8' plus Nazard 2⅔' plus Piccolo 2'

A solo reed may also serve as fundamental in combination with higher octave or mutation registers. See Charts III and IV (pp. 38-39) for further solo possibilities.

The synthetic solo registrations are especially suited for more active and highly figured melodic lines in the soprano voice. The 1⅗' and 1⅓' registers are used *only* in solo combinations that include an 8' fundamental. They are never used in plenum registrations.

*Background Registrations.* The organ frequently functions as an accompanying instrument.[1] It is called on to accompany and serve as background to vocal solos, choral anthems, solo instruments, ensembles, and more frequently, to its own solo registrations. Much of what follows applies equally to each of the above situations. The organist chooses less aggressive, less obtrusive registers from the Flute and Gedackt families to serve as background accompaniment. Background registration will include at least the fundamental 8' pitch so that the notated pitches are actually heard. If the pedal is to be part of the background, it will also have an 8' pitch, often including the octave below, a softer 16' rank.

Balance between a solo registration and its accompaniment must be carefully considered. Should the content of the composition be such that a very gentle solo is desired—such as a Salicional 8' with Nazard 2⅔'—an 8' Gedackt might well suffice as the background. A more intense solo voice, instrument, or register will call for a more intense accompaniment. Again, it will be most satisfying to increase the accompanimental support with the addition of adjacently pitched ranks, not more 8' stops.

Gedackt 8' plus Gemshorn 4'
Gedackt 8' plus Gemshorn 4' plus Hohlfoete 2'
Gedackt 8' plus Gemshorn 4' plus Nazard 2⅔' plus Waldfloete 2'
The pedal support would be increased in like manner:
Subbass 16' plus Rohrfloete 8'
Subbass 16' plus Rohrfloete 8' plus Gemshorn 4'

The accompaniment should never be overly subdued, for often it is in the accompaniment of the solo that the composer portrays the real "essay" on the theme. A fine balance taking into account the content of each part must be attained.

On our sample organ (see Charts III and IV, pp. 38-39) the broad selection of octaves and mutation on the Positiv offer many solo possibilities, especially when both Rohrpfeife 8' and Cromorne 8' are

---

[1]Certainly the most important aspect of this special activity of the organ takes place as it accompanies the congregation in its singing of hymns. This aspect of accompaniment will be discussed under Plenum Registration.

present to serve as fundamental ranks. Examples 1 through 13 indicate possible solos on the Positiv with accompaniment on Great and Pedal. Numbers 2 through 7 use the Rohrpfeife as fundamental, numbers 8 through 13 the Cromorne. Number 7 is an example of the complete Cornet (Kornay or Kornet). Though comprising all flue pipes, the classic combination of 8′, 4′, 2⅔′, 2′, and 1⅗′ has a definite reedy quality.

Numbers 1, 2, and 3 include solos of a rather quiet nature accompanied by the Great Gedackt 8′ alone. The Great coupler to Pedal was drawn in this instance since the Pedal Flachfloete proved too aggressive at the 8′ pitch. Numbers 14 through 18 show a few possibilities for solos on the Great organ. The Fagott, with or without some of the upper ranks (number 16, 17, 18), would provide the most aggressive solo combinations on the organ and would need to be supported by a rather intense Positiv combination including the Principal 2′.

The String family of registers with its more incisive timbre is less successful in background roles. On occasion one might find use for the following combinations as background:

Salicional 8′ plus Celeste 8′
Salicional 8′ plus Rohrfloete 4′

If the range of the accompaniment is rather low, Gedackts and Flutes tend to sound thick and less distinct. String tone might prove cleaner in such cases.

For very intense Trumpet ensembles it will be necessary to draw a Principal rank for adequate support. For background to a combination of Trumpet 8′, Octave 4′, and Mixture III, one might need Diapason 8′, Gemshorn 4′, and Hohlfloete 2′.

*Plenum Registration.* A great number of organ compositions require a mixed-tone and mixed-pitch combination of registers. In this type of composition no single part of the texture is intended by the composer to be emphasized above the other parts. All parts are to be "colored" equally since all are equal in importance. These would include compositions such as fugues, fughettas, canzonas, hymns, hymn settings, and all compositions in harmonic style that have a melody in the topmost voice supported by a chordal or contrapuntal texture. In order that all voices be colored equally, both hands remain on the same manual. Since all parts are equally important, the combination of registers selected should be clear and cohesive. To attain clarity in this type of composition it is especially important to select only one rank of each pitch.

Several requirements for plenum registration follow:

1. A plenum will consist of at least two differently pitched ranks.
2. The highest pitched stop, which is the most easily heard timbre and colors the entire ensemble, should be a Principal register (Principal 4'; Principal, Octave, or Fifteenth 2'; or Mixture).
3. The lowest pitched register will produce the notated pitch, therefore an 8' stop. A 16' plus 8' stop will supply the normal doubled bass foundation for plenum registration in the pedal. If possible, the highest pitched register in the pedal should be a Principal (Principal 8', Choralbass 4', or Octave 4').
4. All octave pitches should be present between the foundation and the highest pitch. Intermediate pitched stops, such as the 2⅔' Quinte may be included between the 4' and 2' Principal ranks.

| | | | | |
|---|---|---|---|---|
| Principal 8' | Principal 4' | | | |
| Gedackt 8' | Principal 4' | | | |
| Gedackt 8' | Principal 4' | Octave 2 ' | | |
| Gedackt 8' | Principal 4' | Quinte 2⅔' | Octave 2' | |
| Gedackt 8' | Rohrfloete 4' | Principal 2 ' | | |

The fullest, most aggressive plenum would make use of all Principal ranks:

| | | | | |
|---|---|---|---|---|
| Principal 8' | Octave 4' | Quinte 2⅔' | Super Octave 2' | Mixture IV |

If Principals are not available at all these pitches, Gedackts or Open Flutes might be substituted.

It is possible to augment or replace the lowest unison and octave pitches in the tonal spectrum with stops of the reed family.

Many of the larger organ builders today follow construction principles of earlier centuries, which specified that each division of the organ be completely independent, including the pedal division. The pedal division was allotted a sufficient number of ranks of the Principal and Gedackt families so that manual to pedal couplers were unnecessary. An independent pedal supporting a large manual plenum would call for Principal ranks at 16', 8', and 4' pitches. The 8' and especially the 4' ranks in the pedal added clarity and distinction to the bass lines, which, of course, is highly desirable in contrapuntal compositions.

Open Principal pipes at 16' and 8' are rather expensive, however, and therefore are not frequently found in smaller organs. 16' and 8' pedal ranks in smaller instruments are therefore most often of the Gedackt family. A 4' Principal, Octave, or Choralebass is frequently included in the pedal division. This 4' Principal tone is often all that is needed to bring a satisfactory degree of precision and the necessary aggressiveness to support a moderate plenum.

If Principals are lacking in the pedal division, a manual to pedal coupler (at 8') must be drawn to gain the desired balance. One sacrifices a degree of clarity and independence in the bass line in so doing, however.

In Chart V (p. 40), "Examples of Plenum Registration," note that the highest pitched rank in each case is the Principal family, either Principal 4', Principal 2', or Mixture III. In all the examples given, each octave between the lowest and highest rank is represented. Further, in each example only one stop of each pitch class is represented, with the exception of the very intense plenum in which an 8' reed duplicates an 8' flue rank.

Examples 1, 2, and 3 are of plenum on the Positiv and Pedal divisions only. Examples 4 through 7 show plenum on the Great organ accompanied by plenum in the Pedal.

Examples 8 through 14 include possible plenums in which Great and Positiv divisions of the organ are coupled. It should be noted, however, that if it is necessary, as in many larger works, to use the second manual for a contrasting dynamic level, the lower pitches on the Positiv manual (8' or 8' and 4') would certainly be drawn to provide the necessary fundamental pitches.

Examples 11 and 12, with Flute ranks at both 8' and 4', pitch levels would produce a more lucid and transparent plenum.

Example 15 denotes a possible use of a reed register as foundation (in place of the flue ranks) in both manual and pedal.

Plenum registrations are used in contrapuntal and harmonic textures in which all voices are equally important. This would include the accompaniment of the hymns and the music of the liturgy. A fine plenum with sturdy, clear Principals is therefore an absolute prerequisite for every church organ.

*Trio and Due Registration.* An organ trio is a composition constructed in three parts throughout. All three parts are independent and relatively equal both melodically and rhythmically. A registration is selected to reflect this particular texture. Using two manuals and uncoupled pedal, the organist registers the three voices with equal intensity but with each part distinct in color and/or pitch emphasis.

In smaller organs particularly, one gains contrast by color only, pitting individual stops of different families against each other. A softer reed stop on one manual against an 8' Flute on the other with an 8' Gemshorn in the pedal might work rather well to give distinction to each of the parts. A Viola da Gamba could well be used against an 8' Gedackt or against a 4' Flute played an octave lower.

On many instruments it may be possible to gain contrast with combinations of registers, each manual including an 8' fundamental of the Gedackt or Flute families plus one or more of the higher octave or mutation ranks. Greatest contrast may be achieved if one manual uses only octave pitches (i.e., 8' + 4' or 8' + 2'), while the other manual includes some non-octave mutation (i.e., 8' + 2⅔'). In trio performance the manual played by the right hand is registered with the highest pitched stop.

The pedal in trio registration is registered to reflect its relative importance in the overall texture. If it is of less interest than the manual parts, it may be sufficient to use only a single 8' Gedackt rank or perhaps 16' plus 8'. More interesting pedal lines might call for 8' plus 4'; or 16' plus 8' plus 4'; possible also is 8' plus 2' or 8' plus 4' plus 2'.

There are a number of fine organ compositions in trio texture in which the pedal carries a *cantus firmus,* the prime melody (usually a chorale tune) on which the entire composition is based. In such cases the two manual voices are balanced in intensity and contrasted in color as above, but the bass voice, carrying the more important melodic line, is given out with an 8' reed or some other more distinctive combination more intense than the two accompanying parts.

Most chorale preludes written in the 17th and 18th centuries come down to us without suggested registrations. Many of the modern editions of these early works, for the sake of authenticity and faithfulness to the original score, likewise leave the matters of registration to the performer. Without the composer's or editor's suggestions, the organist is compelled to consider the music itself—its texture, style, and voice placement among other things—to gain some clue as to the composer's intentions.

On reading through Walther's chorale prelude on "Erhalt uns, Herr, bei deinem Wort," one becomes aware of the consistent three-part texture, the upper two parts reflecting each other melodically and rhythmically. The cantus firmus, in longer note values, appears in the lower staff. This alone might suggest the possibility of a trio registration. The superimposition and crossing of parts in the upper voices in measures 12 and 16 of this excerpt provide further indication that the composition was very likely intended to be played with each hand on a separate manual.

Furthermore, one must determine whether the cantus firmus that appears in the lower staff was intended to be heard as the true bass or whether the composer intended it to be heard between the upper voices as an alto melody supported by the left-hand bass part, which is possible if we assign the pedal voice a 4′ pitch. The upper two voices, especially after the introduction of the pedal part, lie very close to each other in soprano and alto range. The middle voice is quite melodic, hardly in a range or in the character of a bass. In this instance an 8′ register, somewhat more telling than the manual voices, seems the answer. An additional 16′ in the pedal would tend to create a still greater gulf between the alto and Walther's composed bass part.

# Erhalt uns, Herr, bei deinem Wort

(Cantus firmus im Baß)

JOHANN GOTTFRIED WALTHER, 1684-1748

# Further Considerations on the Disposition of Registers

Variation IV of Walther's excellent set of preludes on the chorale "Jesu, meine Freude" presents yet another challenge for the practicing organist. Generally it has four-part texture throughout with the cantus firmus once again presented in the pedal clef. Playing through just the manual parts, one notes that a rather large span separates the upper and lower manual parts generally throughout. The dropping octave, so frequently found in bass parts in organ compositions of this period, is observed in several measures of the left hand (3, 6, 8, 9, 10, 11, and 12). The left-hand part is assigned the root of the chords on most of the stronger beats, and especially at the cadences it provides the roots for the authentic cadences (V—I). These facts should indicate to the organist that the pedal cantus firmus was meant to be performed *above* the left hand part. A 4′ register in the pedal division would present this chorale theme for the most part between the right hand and left hand parts, filling in the space that existed there; at the same time it would allow the left-hand part to remain as the lowest sounding voice—the true bass.

It would be necessary to assign the cantus firmus a reed or chorale bass at that 4′ pitch to assure a degree of prominence from within the accompanying voices. The hand parts should be played on the same manual with a quieter background registration.

## Jesu, meine Freude

JOHANN GOTTFRIED WALTHER, 1684-1748

The pedal can be used quite advantageously to bring out chorale themes that might otherwise be lost in a maze of contrapuntal interweaving. If the pedal division lacks solo possibilities at 8' or at 4', it might well be possible to couple one of the manual solo ranks to the pedal using the other manual as accompaniment.

Georg Telemann's lovely prelude on the Communion hymn "Schmücke dich, o liebe Seele" was originally written with the cantus firmus on the manual staff between two accompanying voices:

## Schmücke dich, o liebe Seele
### (Cantus firmus im Tenor)

GEORG PHILIPP TELEMANN, 1681-1767

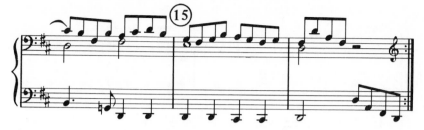

If performed with the hands alone as the score seems to suggest, the chorale is completely subdued and for the most part unheard by even the most attentive listener. Though written in this manner, it is quite probable that the composer intended that the chorale theme be assigned a solo registration to give it the prominence it deserves. The solo could be performed on a solo register played by the left hand with the lowest voice then performed by the pedals. It might more easily be performed with the solo tenor chorale played on an 8′ solo register on the pedals with both accompanying parts played on a manual with a background registration.

## Schmücke dich, o liebe Seele

GEORG PHILIPP TELEMANN, 1681-1767

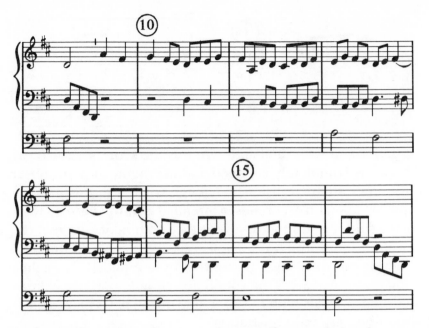

A change in registration or a change of manuals in plenum compositions will often help delineate sections within a larger composition, clarifying the overall form for the listener. Contrasting plenum registrations might well be used in the following prelude by Richard Hillert.

## Let Us Ever Walk with Jesus

Richard Hillert

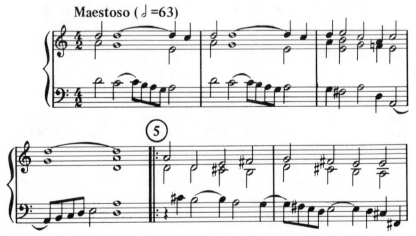

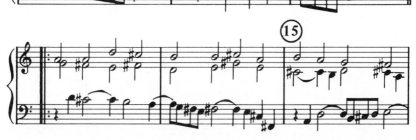

33

After a brief fanfarelike introduction, measure 5 introduces the first phrase of the Chorale. Thereafter phrases of the chorale alternate with four-measure interludes related to the opening gesture. The over-all form is much like a little rondo. Though the texture is quite similar throughout, some contrast in registration, be it ever so slight, will help bring the relationship of the parts in focus with the fanfare sections one plenum, the chorale sections on another.

Thinner-textured episodic passages in larger works, especially of the baroque masters, often call for lighter plenum registrations on a secondary manual.

# Praeludium
### pro Organo pleno

J.S.BACH, 1685-1750

The superscription "pro Organo pleno" was frequently used by the composers of this era to indicate a basic plenum registration: Principals 8′, 4′, 2′, and Mixture. Though this is a very short prelude, it does provide us with an example of the type of episodic passage that might well be executed on a secondary manual. After an initial statement, principally structured on a descending six-note motive, a strong authentic cadence arrives in measures 8 and 9. The sequential patterns in measures 9 through 15 introduce a thinner texture with three voices of a more transitory nature. This brief modulatory passage, less imposing than the opening statement, acts as a buffer between the C major and the a minor statement that appears again in measure 16. Passages of this nature (episodic, transitory, often modulatory) function best on a secondary manual at a reduced plenum.

Many of the larger baroque organ preludes, toccatas, and concerti were conceived in the concerto grosso style, alternating between "tutti" (larger ensemble) and "concertino" (smaller ensemble of soloists). In these organ compositions thicker, more imposing sections were contrasted with thinner-textured sections, calling for movement between the primary and the secondary manuals of the organ. Gaining intensification in registration in these longer alternating compositions, was done by adding registers judiciously so that at each return the manual is somewhat brighter.

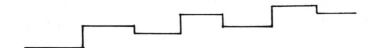

# Mechanical Registrational Devices

*Swell Shutters.* The position of the Swell shutters seriously affects the color of the selected registration. Closing the shutters with the use of the swell pedal diminishes greatly the distinctive color, especially the upper, lighter overtones of the sounding registers. The normal position of the swell is open, for it allows the true color of the pipe tone to reach the listener without distortion. In order to reduce volume the organist should first consider the subtraction of stops. The most artistic use of the Swell pedal, which controls the swell shutters, should be to achieve gentle nuance rather than dramatic change in volume. Stainton Taylor comments:

> The organist may well bear this fact in mind when tempted to keep his foot planted on the swell pedal, and remember that generally Bach's music sounds just as well without its use. Yet it would be as foolish to forswear the swell pedal altogether as to refuse to use pistons or tone colors in the modern organ which were unknown to Bach and his predecessors. The really sensitive player will know how to use it in such a way as to heighten the appeal of many passages in the chorale preludes.[1]

*Tremulants.* Tremulants, if gentle and unobtrusive, may be used with individual or synthetic combination solo registers. The organist would best be on guard against excessive use of this device. Tremulants are never to be used with larger combinations and most certainly not in the accompaniments of hymns or in the accompanying of the music of the liturgy where sturdiness of tone is much desired.

*The Register Crescendo.* The Register Crescendo became rather popular on the organs of the last century and is still included in many of the organs in present use. The Register Crescendo is operated by a pedal lever that, when depressed gradually, adds the stops in order from the softest to the loudest, often including the manual 16′ stops as well as upper and lower couplers. The overall effect may provide

[1]Stainton Taylor, *The Chorale Preludes of J. S. Bach* (London: Oxford University Press, 1941).

36

a most powerfully resounding tone but hardly provides the clarity and precision that most organ music requires. Stainton Taylor again states: "We are quite justified in looking upon it [the crescendo pedal] as a dangerous toy so far as the music of Bach is concerned." Of course, there are occasions when it can be quite effective. The music of the late Romantic composers, especially Max Reger, provides opportunity for its use. The inclusion of 16' manual stops, sub couplers, and super couplers in this mechanism renders it totally out of place in the accompaniment of hymns and the music of the liturgy.

# Appendix A

Solo registrations are shown by reading down the chart by column. For example, solo registration 1 consists of 8′ Gedackt (Manual I), 8′ Cromorne (Manual II), 16′ Subbass (Pedal), and Great—Pedal Coupler.

| | 1 | 2 | 3 | 4 | 5 | 6 | 7 | 8 | 9 | 10 | 11 | 12 | 13 | |
|---|---|---|---|---|---|---|---|---|---|---|---|---|---|---|
| **Manual I (Great)** | | | | | | | | | | | | | | |
| Gedackt 8′ | x | x | x | x | x | x | x | x | x | x | x | x | x | |
| Principal 4′ | | | | | | | | | | | | | | |
| Spitzfloete 4′ | | | | x | x | x | x | x | x | x | x | x | x | |
| Hohlfloete 2′ | | | | | | | | | | | | | | |
| Mixture III | | | | | | | | | | | | | | |
| Fagott 8′ | | | | | | | | | | | | | | |
| **Manual II (Positiv)** | | | | | | | | | | | | | | |
| Rohrpfeife 8′ | | x | x | x | x | x | x | | | | | | | |
| Gemshorn 4′ | | | x | | | x | x | | | x | x | x | x | |
| Principal 2′ | | | | | | | x | | | | | | | |
| Nasat 2⅔′ | | x | | | x | x | x | x | | x | | x | x | |
| Terz 1⅗′ | | | x | x | x | x | | | x | | x | x | | |
| Cromorne 8′ | x | | | | | | x | x | x | x | x | x | | |
| **Pedal** | | | | | | | | | | | | | | |
| Subbass 16′ | x | x | x | x | x | x | x | x | x | x | x | x | | |
| Flachfloete 8′ | | | | x | x | x | x | x | x | x | x | x | x | |
| Lab. Dulcian 4′ | | | | | | | | | | | | | | |
| Nachthorn 2′ | | | | | | | | | | | | | | |
| Fagott 16′ | | | | | | | | | | | | | | |
| Cromorne 4′ | | | | | | | | | | | | | | |
| **Couplers** | | | | | | | | | | | | | | |
| Great—Pedal | x | x | x | | | | | | | | | | | |
| Pos.—Pedal | | | | | | | | | | | | | | |
| Pos.—Great | | | | | | | | | | | | | | |

**Chart III — Solo (Positiv) with Accompaniment**

| | 14 | 15 | 16 | 17 | 18 | 19 | 20 | 21 | 22 | 23 | 24 | 25 | | | |
|---|---|---|---|---|---|---|---|---|---|---|---|---|---|---|---|
| **Manual I (Great)** | | | | | | | | | | | | | | | |
| Gedackt 8' | x | x | | | | x | x | x | x | | x | x | | | |
| Principal 4' | | | x | x | | | | | | | | | | | |
| Spitzfloete 4' | x | | | | | | | | | | x | x | | | |
| Hohlfloete 2' | | x | | | | | | | | | | | | | |
| Mixture III | | | | | x | | | | | | | | | | |
| Fagott 8' | | | x | x | x | | | | | | | | | | |
| **Manual II (Positiv)** | | | | | | | | | | | | | | | |
| Rohrpfeife 8' | x | x | x | x | x | | | | | x | | | | | |
| Gemshorn 4' | | | x | x | x | | | | | x | | | | | |
| Principal 2' | | | x | x | x | | | | | | | | | | |
| Nasat 2⅔' | | | | | x | | | | | | | | | | |
| Terz 1⅗' | | | | | | | | | | | | | | | |
| Cromorne 8' | | | | | | | | | x | | | | | | |
| **Pedal** | | | | | | | | | | | | | | | |
| Subbass 16' | x | x | x | x | x | | | | | | | | | | |
| Flachfloete 8' | | | x | x | x | | | | | | x | x | | | |
| Lab. Dulcian 4' | | | x | x | x | | | x | | x | | x | | | |
| Nachthorn 2' | | | | x | | | x | | | x | | | | | |
| Fagott 16' | | | | | | | | | | | | | | | |
| Cromorne 4' | | | | | | x | x | | | | x | | | | |
| **Couplers** | | | | | | | | | | | | | | | |
| Great—Pedal | | | | | | | | | | | | | | | |
| Pos.—Pedal | x | x | | | | | | | x | | | | | | |
| Pos.—Great | | | | | | | | | | | | | | | |

**Chart IV — Solo with Accompaniment**
**Solo on Great (14–18)**
**Solo on Pedal (19–25)**

| | 1 | 2 | 3 | 4 | 5 | 6 | 7 | 8 | 9 | 10 | 11 | 12 | 13 | 14 | 15 |
|---|---|---|---|---|---|---|---|---|---|---|---|---|---|---|---|
| **Manual I (Great)** | | | | | | | | | | | | | | | |
| Gedackt 8' | | | | x | x | x | x | x | x | x | x | x | x | x | |
| Principal 4' | | | | x | x | x | x | x | x | x | | | | x | x |
| Spitzfloete 4' | | | | | | | | | | | x | x | x | | |
| Hohlfloete 2' | | | | | | x | | | | | | | | | |
| Mixture III | | | | | x | x | x | | x | x | | | | x | x | x |
| Fagott 8' | | | | | | x | | | | | | | x | x | x |
| **Manual II (Positiv)** | | | | | | | | | | | | | | | |
| Rohrpfeife 8' | x | x | x | | | | | | | | | | | | |
| Gemshorn 4' | x | x | x | | | | | | | | | | | | |
| Principal 2' | x | x | x | | | | | x | x | x | x | x | x | x | x |
| Nasat 2⅔' | | x | x | | | | | | x | | x | | x | x |
| Terz 1⅗' | | | | | | | | | | | | | | | |
| Cromorne 8' | | x | | | | | | | | | | | | | |
| **Pedal** | | | | | | | | | | | | | | | |
| Subbass 16' | x | x | x | x | x | x | x | x | | | x | x | x | x | |
| Flachfloete 8' | | | | x | x | x | x | x | | | x | x | x | x | x |
| Lab. Dulcian 4' | | | | | x | x | x | | | | x | x | x | x | x |
| Nachthorn 2' | | | | | | x | | | | | | | | x | x |
| Fagott 16' | | | | | | | x | | | | | | x | x | x |
| Cromorne 4' | | | | | | | | | | | | | | | |
| **Couplers** | | | | | | | | | | | | | | | |
| Great—Pedal | | | | | | | | | | | | | | | |
| Pos.—Pedal | x | x | x | | | | | | | | | | | | |
| Pos.—Great | | | | | | | | x | x | x | x | x | x | x | |

# Chart V — Examples of Plenum Registration

# Appendix B

(Reprinted from Carl Halter and Carl Schalk, eds., *A Handbook of Church Music* [St. Louis: Concordia Publishing House, 1978], pp. 177–82. Used by permission.)

## Classification of Organ Pipes

According to the manner of tone production, organ pipes are of two types: *labial* or *flue*, in which the tone is produced by the impact of a stream of air upon a sharp liplike upper edge of the mouth; and *lingual* or *reed*, in which a metal reed is the sound-producing agent. Within each type the tone of different stops will vary according to such factors as the scale of the pipes (ratio of diameter to length); whether the shape of the pipe is cylindrical, conical, or tapered; whether the top of the pipe is open, covered, or partly covered; and the width and shape of the mouth.

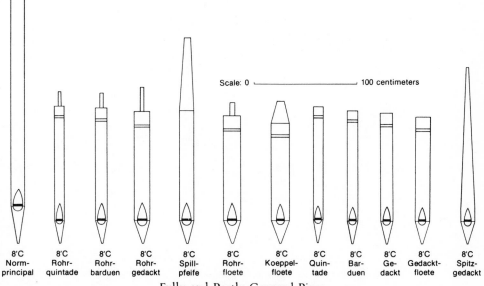

Scale: 0 ⎣————————————⎦ 100 centimeters

| 8'C Norm-principal | 8'C Rohr-quintade | 8'C Rohr-barduen | 8'C Rohr-gedackt | 8'C Spill-pfeife | 8'C Rohr-floete | 8'C Koeppel-floete | 8'C Quin-tade | 8'C Bar-duen | 8'C Ge-dackt | 8'C Gedackt-floete | 8'C Spitz-gedackt |

Fully and Partly Covered Pipes

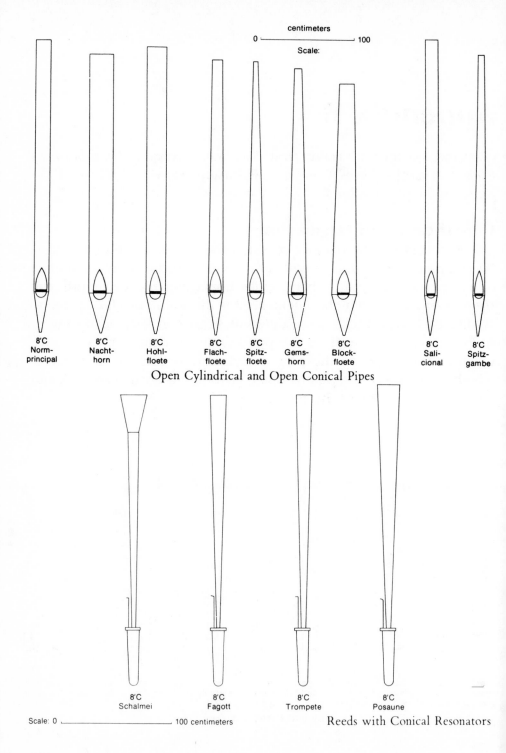

centimeters

0 ⊢————————⊣ 100

Scale:

| 8'C Norm-principal | 8'C Nacht-horn | 8'C Hohl-floete | 8'C Flach-floete | 8'C Spitz-floete | 8'C Gems-horn | 8'C Block-floete | 8'C Sali-cional | 8'C Spitz-gambe |

## Open Cylindrical and Open Conical Pipes

| 8'C Schalmei | 8'C Fagott | 8'C Trompete | 8'C Posaune |

Scale: 0 ⊢————————⊣ 100 centimeters

## Reeds with Conical Resonators

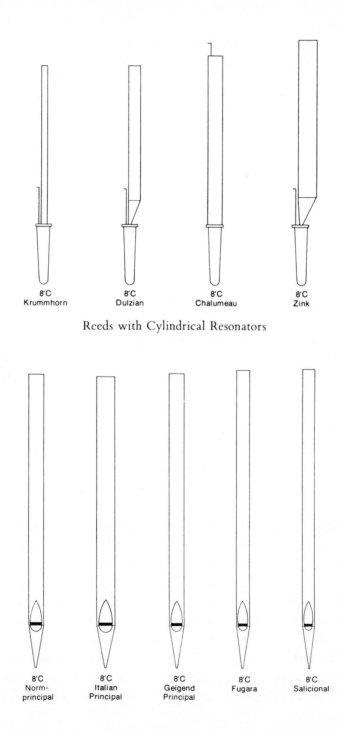

8'C
Krummhorn

8'C
Dulzian

8'C
Chalumeau

8'C
Zink

Reeds with Cylindrical Resonators

8'C
Norm-
principal

8'C
Italian
Principal

8'C
Geigend
Principal

8'C
Fugara

8'C
Salicional

## Labial Pipes

Traditionally, labial pipes have been divided into two major classifications and a minor one: Class I or Principal, Class II or Gedackt-Flute, and the Strings.

The Principal pipes supply the most basic organ tone, the tone that forms the supporting backbone of the instrument. Principal tone is full, rich, and aggressive throughout the entire range. When the various pitches at which it is present are combined, the resulting ensemble has a blend and clarity that is ideal for contrapuntal music. This class of pipes is also known as "Diapason," although this term may imply the thicker and heavier type of tone found in organs from the earlier part of this century. The principal pipes also provide the normal scale, the standard against which other classes of pipes are described as either wide or narrow.

Principal stops will be represented at 16', 8', 4', 2⅔', and 2' pitches as well as in the mixtures. According to design logic the lowest pitch at which this class is present in a division is given the name Principal. The remaining stops receive names that describe their pitch relation to this principal: Octave, Quint, or Twelfth; Octavin, Super-Octave, or Fifteenth. This practice is not carried out consistently in the naming of stops on all instruments. English organs frequently designated the 4' rank as Principal even when the class was represented at a lower pitch in that division. Modifications in the basic structure or scale of principal pipes are sometimes indicated by prefixes such as Italian-, Geigen-, Violin-, Harfen-, Spitz-, or Weit-.

Gedackt pipes of Class II are covered or stopped at the top. Because a stopped pipe produces a tone an octave lower than an open pipe of the same length, such pipes need be only half their stated pitch length. Hence, there is a saving in space and material when 16' and 8' stops are covered rather than open. The basic tonal characteristic of Gedackt pipes is a somewhat hollow sound due to the presence of only odd-numbered harmonics in a stopped pipe. This sound serves as an excellent foundation when combined with stops of higher pitches. Gedackts include Untersatz and Subbass 16'; Gedackt, Pommer, Bourdon, and Quintation at 16' and 8' and occasionally 4'; and Stopped Diapason 8'.

Related to the Gedackt pipes are the partly covered pipes, in which the cover or stopper of the pipe is pierced with a narrow open cylindrical tube or chimney extending upwards. Such registers, generally found at either 8' or 4', can be recognized by the prefix Rohr- or Chimney-: Rohrfloete, Rohrbourdon, Chimney Flute. Also belonging to the partly covered group would be two stops generally found at 4', Spillfloete and Koppelfloete; the partial covering is achieved by having a cylindrical section of pipe topped by a section that tapers to a much small opening.

Flute pipes are open, full-length, and generally have a fuller tone than the Gedackts since all the harmonics are present. Included would be cylindrical pipes at 4' and 2' such as Nachthorn and Hohlfloete, tapered pipes such as Spitzfloete and Gemshorn at 8' and 4', and the Blockfloete, Waldfloete, and Flachfloete at 4' and 2'. Mutations at 2⅔', 1⅗', and 1⅓' are frequently of this type.

A special group of labial or flue pipes of lesser importance than the above two classes are the string stops. These have a narrower scale, a thinner and more cutting tone. Less suited to contrapuntal and rapid passages, they find their value in chordal passages where their peculiar sonority is a desired feature. They include Viola da Gamba, Salicional, Viola, Spitzgamba, and Dulciana. A special effect produced with string stops should also be noted. The term celeste refers to a second string stop which is tuned slightly higher or lower than the first one of this type; the resulting beats from the variation in tuning add an undulating effect to the ensemble that is pleasing in certain softer registrations. The celeste should never be used in contrapuntal passages nor in combination with more than a single 8' or 4' stop.

## Reed Pipes

As a class, the reed stops have the greatest variety of tone color and brilliance and may, if desired, also have the greatest amount of weight and volume of all the registers on the organ. The length of the tone-producing agent, the thin metal reed, regulated by a tuning wire, is the principal influence on the pitch, while the shape and length of the resonator or pipe body has the greatest effect on the tone quality. Reeds are divided into three groups according to the shape of the resonators.

Pipes with conical resonators from this group include the reeds that are most commonly found on organs. They may be used both as solo stops and to add a capstone brilliance to the full ensemble. The basic stop is the 8' Trumpet; when used at 4' it is usually called Clarion; at 16' Posaune or Bombarde. The Fagott is generally found at 16' and 8' pitches and the Oboe or Hautbois at 8'.

Pipes with cylindrical resonators have an effect similar to that of stopped labial pipes—reinforcing only the odd-number harmonics. The resulting tone is thin and also somewhat hollow sounding. The most common registers in this group are the Dulzian at 16' or 8', Krummhorn 8', Clarinet 8', and Rohrschalmei 8' or 4'.

Pipes with fractional length resonators are of many different shapes leading to the greatest variety of tone color. Most commonly found are the Vox Humana, Rankett, and all kinds of Regals. German prefixes are often attached to the term regal; consultation with a dictionary will show that these are terms that describe the shape of the resonator: cone, knob, sphere, funnel, etc.

# Bibliography

Barnes, William H. *The Contemporary American Organ.* New York: J. Fischer and Bro.

Gleason, Harold. *Method of Organ Playing.* New York: Appleton-Century-Crofts, Inc., 1949.

Gotsch, Herbert. "The Organ in the Lutheran Service of the 16th Century." *Church Music,* 1967, no. 1:7–12.

Halter, Carl. *The Practice of Sacred Music.* St. Louis: Concordia Publishing House, 1955.

Halter, Carl, and Carl Schalk, eds. *A Handbook of Church Music.* St. Louis: Concordia Publishing House, 1978.

Jamison, James B. *Organ Design and Appraisal.* New York: H. W. Gray, 1950.

Johnson, David N. *Instruction Book for Beginning Organists.* Minneapolis: Augsburg Publishing House, 1964.

Koch, Casper. *The Organ Students Gradus ad Parnassum.* New York: J. Fischer and Bro., 1945.

Luedtke, Charles H. *Fundamentals of Organ Registration.* New Ulm, Minn.: Dr. Martin Luther College Press, n.d.

Phelps, Lawrence I. "A Short History of the Organ Revival." *Church Music,* 1967, no. 1:13–30.

# Acknowledgments

From Charles Luedtke, *Fundamentals of Organ Registration*: Chart I.

From Edition Peters 4448 (*80 Chorale Preludes*): "Erhalt uns, Herr, bei deinem Wort." Used by permission.

From Flor Peeters, *Ars organi* [Brussels: Schott Freres], part 1, adapted: Chart II. Used with the permission of SCHOTT FRERE Edition, Brussels-Paris.

From *Organ Music for the Communion Service*, © 1956 Concordia Publishing House: "Schmücke dich," three-staff version. Used by permission.

From *The Parish Organist: Wedding Music*, part 9, © 1962 Concordia Publishing House: "Let Us Ever Walk with Jesus." Used by permission.

From *Walthers Orgelchoräle*, Bärenreiter #379: "Jesu, meine Freude." Used by permission.